Fleeting Feels

Floating Feelings...

Fleeting Feels

Floating Feelings...

Dr. Kum Kum Ray

EXCELLER BOOKS®
A GLOBAL PRESS

Fleeting Feels
Floating Feelings...

Cover design by Exceller Books

ISBN: 978-93-47397-21-9

Published in India in 2025 by Exceller Books,
An imprint of GE Group,
G1, Dream Apartment, Degree College Road, Belgharia,
Kolkata, 700056, India
www.excellerbooks.com

EXCELLER BOOKS®
A GLOBAL PRESS

The Divine in serenity

&

dear ones

Foreword

What a delightful yet welcoming burden, to be asked to frame someone else's heart as it taps across the page—especially when that heart belongs to one's mother. What can a foreword do, really? Offer a peek: come in, hush now, see how the dust hangs expectantly in the play of the light? *Fleeting Feelings; Enduring Memories* slips us notes folded by a life lived in contradictions: dust to dust, mountain to mountain, the infinite pressed close by worn familial hands, ritual and rebellion waltzing the length of each poem—all capturing, in some part, the journey of my mother.

Here, lineage isn't a soft genealogy but a fiery root shooting through bureaucracy and sal woods, muggy Deccan evenings, the Holy Ganga's brimming embankment, and a convent's whispering chapel. The wit is infused steeply with grief, refusing the easy adjectives of loss—preferring to wear absence as a second skin, or sometimes as the sari's border fraying just so, familiar and unfinished.

My mother writes as if every poem is the lighter's flick before lighting a cigarette for a chain smoker: the ancestors staring from their portraits, children and grandchildren tumbling about the house, the river outside insisting on its own endlessness.

Her voice drifts between goddess and grandmother, lover and teacher, always, I suspect, in toothy dialogue with the gods. Who else but my mother, a Professor of Literature, would snipe at the infinite, toss the bouquet to Marx, let Ginsberg haunt Kashi at ninety-four—all while worrying if the rice will be done before the guests arrive?

To read these poems is to find one eye on the mirror, unsure if the reflection winks or weeps; one finger pressed to the pulse of land, family, the rustle of a file dusting itself to eternity; a mother's sari that contains so many allegorical references anyway; the beautiful symphony of a monsoon tirade hitting a tin roof and petrichor rising from the ground up.

The wife in her hands us contradictions—detachment knotted tight to ferocious belonging, the holiness of the mundane, *nishkaam karm* looping through the chaos of the everyday. The woman of the world makes the everyday stand out as much as the mystical is made to appear ordinary. It is her mischief that has remained with her for seven decades since she was a child.

I implore you to bring your own waves when you open this book. Or if you are scared, feel free to borrow hers: the garrulous rivers, widowhood's threnodies, colours falling from the trees, the daily grind's refrain, and a perennial hunger for justice—a desire to dissolve, at last, into something infinite and kind.

This is not poetry as prettification, but as vital record, as ledger, as the *kalam-dawat* puja scribbled in the margins of living and dying alike.

If these are fleeting feelings, let them refuse to fade: read them aloud, let the dust tickle your throat, hear the quiet that thrums beneath *taal* and traffic, bed and ghat, mother and daughter, the ungovernable world—brief yet endless.

What more can I say?

Her son is in the destiny of her karma,

Rai Mahimapat Ray
Indian Administrative Service (IAS), 2011 Batch
On Deputation with the World Bank

Contents

Philosophies

Silent Thoughts

Infinite & Me

Bow in Gratitude, O Lord!
For making me a speck of dust,
To fly free on the dappled shoulders of leaves, birds, and clouds,
As free as Nature grows… to follow my heart.
Dust I am,
In dust do I live,
To dust I will turn.
All quests ended,
Intermingled in dust with the ashes of what once was my body—
Only the infinite will live on.
Dust around me,
In the grass…
On tree leaves,
Like a thin veil on the flowers,
Waiting to be lifted…
Into the arms of the beloved,
To ride on the winds,
Into the clouds…
Amazement to spiritual attainment.

The thirst of the greens
Seems like the unquenched, unsatisfied soul,
Ever lusting and ever wanting,
Unable to disentangle from the material world,
Unlike the
Dust waiting to be sublimated…
With drops of rain,
Quenched and fulfilled.
Like the dust…
One day,
I will blow across the land and seas;
Tumultuous dunes around me on all sides,
Delusions blind…
Oh! Silent One, come and bring tranquillity and rest.
The *Shunya Purush* (*Bhagavad Gita*),

Awaken my seeing towards this nothingness.

I am a speck, a speck of sand, in this material world…
Where every fragrance awakens desire, the spirit possesses.
I try, dig, digress and divert,
For every single manifestation appears to be changing
In this physical world.

Hold my hand, pull me to envisage immortality in this mortal world;
Merge with me, *Shunya Purush* (*Bhagavad Gita*),
In this luring, living, lively, lonesome,
Lustrous, loathsome world.
The dust from my body be afloat on Ganga Mai's breast.

I

If seeing is believing,
I can see it in your eyes...
If hearing is feeling,
I can feel it in your voice...
If sensation is telling,
Your vibrations tell me...
There is a strange chemistry
That works beyond consciousness,
Pulling us together,
Tearing us apart,
Making us happy,
Each is an incomplete part,
Satisfied with ourselves,
Yet a truncated half,
Longing for togetherness
Even more and more...

If history sets examples,
Then examples do repeat,
Of loved ones torn apart
By societal powers.
Though destiny says otherwise,
For it was destined to be—
Life of my life,
Soul of my soul,
My ecstasy, my sin,
My reason for existence,
My life's goal.

I have felt the pain of separation—
Ask not of whom.
I have felt the pains of absence—
Ask not of whom.
I have given my soul to my beloved;
How does it matter to another?

My Own Religion

I am neither a Shaivite,
Nor a Vaishnavite,
Nor a Hindu,
Nor a Muslim,
Nor to any identified religion belong.
Yet grew up fasting
Every Shivratri,
Believing in the strength of prayers for the conjugal love of one.
Worshipping the Durga
In her nine forms
All through the Navratri,
I discovered in the symbols the strength of womanhood—
In all nine forms of different roles of women.
From *Shailputri* to *Brahmacharini*,
To *Mahishasurmardini*;
All because my mother told me.
But went to church,
Brought up in the Catholic ambience of a convent school.
Introspected in solitude,
Guilt-laden,
Believing that
Those who live by the cross die by the cross...
As age progressed,
Hanumanji became my guardian angel,
The Sufi saints my passion.
With these heady combinations, I made my own self,
Doing unto others
What I wished others to do unto me.
I grew away, a freak believing in myself
And some Supreme Being—non-existent yet all around—
Engraved into my being,
First by my mother, then by the nuns,
And finally I arrived to learn
That my religion is my own,
A concoction difficult to explain or to be understood.

But who cares!
For I am in love
With life—
My cross,
Ethic and values,
Believing in *Nishkaam Karm.*

20th Feb 2007

I am neither a Sita
Nor a Savitri,
Not ever a Mariam or Mary.
I created my mould, struggled and broke from my shell,
Upsetting structured casts,
Disappointing manyfold,
Like one who follows
Her own music,
Which those around find difficult to behold...
Composing songs which may remain unsung,
An amalgamation of rhythms and tunes,
Yet unheard,
Waiting for ears in expectancy.

22nd Feb 2007

The heart weighs heavy with separation.
It would do good if we met.
I don't care for modalities,
How one does it…
Nor seek to answer why one has to do it.
For one to whom you are emotionally bound,
And unto whom you are drawn,
May be gold, may be diamond,
May even be nimble.
How does that matter?

20th Feb 2004

I have felt the pain of separation
Ask not of whom
I have felt the pains of absence
Ask not of whom
I have given my soul to my beloved
How does it matter to another?

Desires

Lay me down where the pines sleep
In the Himalayan lap…
Where freshness one breathes…
Like the hills thrash
That fluttering trees in restlessness…
Then subsides to serenity,
Peaceful as she rests…
Lay me here, if not alive, at least in death…
People may conceive
Here lies she dead,
A loved mother, a dutiful wife,
A doting daughter and a generous grandma.
But the satiated me will live on,
Merged with the winds
That sing in the silver oak tree.
So lay me down in the Queen of Hills…
Denied dwelling when I was alive,
But free in death to roam from what I was made for…
The hungry soul
Likes cloud afloat;
In moment descents
And then rises a bloat,
Pregnant with droplets,
Thought in restless mode:
Take subterfuge amidst hills,
In nature's vibrant code.

Teaching Is My Art

Art, Skill, Profession, Occupation, Vocation pursuits matter.
In minor ways,
How a plant grows,
How a Lily blooms,
How silence spreads…
Silence in the winds,
Silence in the seas,
Silence in the trees,
Silence in the woods,
Silence in the world…
Sneaking around the lethal, hideous…
When silence speaks and struggles for survival,
It is not as minor as it appears;
Not as minor and simple as it seems.
Yet perceptions recognise efforts,
One's conscious effort to perform one's Profession.
My effort is to elevate my professional skills, investing in global research, transitioning boundaries,
Managing knowledge with innovations and grabbing opportunities
With unparalleled expertise;
Attention unlimited.
With our student-centric bonds
Sleeping as the night dawns,
Self-reflecting: "We can do better."
That is what 'my teacher's identity' means to me.
It's not just my job but my 'art'; my pursuit…
Footprints that help the student in their destination, 'success',
Facing turbulent times,
Yet growing and preserving themselves in Humanitarian Mankind.

21st Feb 2007

Women is the root
Man the branches
Children the fruit

And love the flowers
That is if nature is kind…
The root gets shaky when the branches break off
The fruit unpair and fall
And flowers dry away within
That is if nature is variant
The root gets uprooted when branches start drying
The leaves shovel and the pod falls away
This is when nature plays truant
And makes us believe in destiny

II

Every day draws me nearer to death,
Yet every night, I look forward to another dawn.
Every day stretches long,
Bringing weariness, living alone,
Yet not lonely, I move on.
Vacancy surrounds me many a time,
Yet the giggling, stammering words of toddlers,
The clasping of warm, friendly, affectionate hands
Pulls me on.
I wander and wander, sitting underneath a shady bower of fruit-laden trees,
And a host of lilies around,
Ariel, Easter, Peace, Lillian…

III

Sometimes when nothing goes just right
And worry reigns supreme,
When heartache fills the eyes with mist
And all things useless seem,
There's just one thing can drive away
The tears that scald and blind—
Someone to slip a strong arm 'round
And whisper, "Never mind."
No one has ever told just why
Those words such comfort bring;
Nor why that whisper makes our cares
Depart on hurried wing.
Yet troubles say a quick "Good-day,"
We leave them far behind
When someone slips an arm around,
And whispers, "Never mind."
But love must prompt that soft caress—
That love must, aye, be true;
Or at that tender, clinging touch
No heart ease come to you.
But if the arm be moved by love,
Sweet comfort you will find
When someone slips an arm around,
And whispers, "Never mind!"
—Anonymous
Another day,
Another dawn,
Like many before,
A silent morn…

Glimpse and Shadow of Life

The anguish
That ensues
When my children, Dr Mohua, a phantom of a woman; Talish, a logical, outspoken lawyer;
Rai Mahimapati, a compassionate, quiet leader,
Are incandescent, lively, impressive,
Leaving trails of light and robust vigour.
Grandchildren,
When they leave,
It is so challenging, mentally and physically,
Without my partner,
Their father and grandfather.
I can hardly handle it.
Even Hanumanji does not bring solace.
Detachment with attachment
So logical
Does not make sense.
Then commences
The desire to see my journey's end,
Free from attachments.
The body ails.
The eyes cannot hold back tears.
Pacifying no longer works.
Yet, I have to tread
As a weary traveller
On desolate grounds.
Whatever has been a principle undergoes a change in life.
A new way of living is not easy.
Return to simplicity is essential to being, a mind of one's own.
Every shade, every shadow, and glimpse of life past,
Bruises and hurts,
Must come to terms
With my terms.
An ageing, working widow, young in spirit, restless under criticism,
With a vision of a feeble picture,
Essential to *Being*.

Must accept
They cannot live with me
As they did in their childhood.
They have moved on, have tasks to fulfil.
Work hard! We instilled in them the *sanskars*
That we taught as parents.
We were the world, we are the voice.
Do not feel sorry for the dead.
Feel sorry for the ones
They leave behind.
Move on like waves in the Ganges.

Papu 'Paye' – The Father of My Children

(From a Spouse & a Mother)

What would I give to be with you again,
Half a decade is a long time, they say,
Yet five years seem just like yesterday.
What I miss the most, that has left a void, nothing seems to fill;
Was it the depth of emotions you shared?
Was it the rage with which you cared?
Was it the causes you impassioned?
Was it your clairvoyance that always made me wonder, were you a seer?
Was it your wisdom that seemed to know my world more than me?
Was it that you knew more than most, encyclopaedic?
Was it that you could suffer even the pedantic?
Was it that you could connect with anyone who crossed your path?
Was it that you never followed your path because others sought it of you?
Was it because you were a doting father?
Was it for your ability to smile while pacing up and down in your thoughts?
Was it that we rarely agreed, and when we did it was for the wrong reasons?
Was it for the guru who taught me all the right lessons?
Was it because I never learnt all the lessons you had to teach when I had the time?
Was it your unique stories that never ended, till your voice did?
Was it the generosity you espoused with all your means?
Was it wondrous how deep and wide an impact you could be in everyone you met?
The truth for missing you, Papu Paye, I do not know,
My only truth now is that I have thought of you more often than I did when you were in our midst.
I have dreamt of you,
I know you would be laughing at that, since dreams never come true;

They are merely a sign of sleeping too much, you would say.
Yet I have dreamt of you even when I have slept far too little.
I have thought of you,
I have thought of you ever so often.
Sometimes it amazes me how often.
Mostly, though, it leaves me sad that I didn't get enough time with you.
Rare and beautiful is when thoughts of you bring a smile to me.
I have not spoken of you to anyone,
I have not written of you to anyone,
Not because I haven't tried, but because each time I have tried, I have choked.
Half a decade may be a long time, they may say,
I know that the five years have passed by in a blink of an eyelid,
And know that my Papu Paye, you are missed in my life more than you were when you were around.

The Daily Grind

Even today when I can't find motivation or joy in what I am doing,
All I ask myself: Is this the best I can do right now?
That internal compass which guides me to a better self every day?
Just as the Sun moves from the Tropic of Cancer to the Capricorn…
Back again to Cancer,
Does it look for motivation?
It does what it has to do
To keep the Universe going!

Long Live Mahoua

If I cease to breathe...
Creature of an hour, I am not an island.
Like everyone, I am a piece of humanity.
Like any creature of this kind, planet,
I float, swim, kicking in the dark sea,
Reaching out to the sunlight...
Before my eyes, illumination stares,
My Mahoua blooming...
A canopy of pure white flowers bathed in the moonlit sky.
As the morn dawns...
With the sun,
I see Mahoua spread out like a carpet on earth,
Being picked by poor locals
For its sweet taste...
Seasoning it
For intoxication's spur.
My autumn is in diminishing years,
Yet October takes me back to my youthful mother's days,
Cause Mahoua came in my lap,
And I shared her with mankind for pain to cease...

To a Son/Sun from Mummy

With every sunrise: every sunset,
My faith tells me you were in my destiny.
Destined for us: Kum Kum & Umapati entwined.
My son, my very own.
Our affections bounce from me to you,
You to me.
As long as I breathe, you will be in my arms,
In my prayers,
In my blessings.

A Widows Voice

The Father of My Children
There is none like you
A brilliant visionary:
A guru, so wise; so informative, logical…
Drawing people around with generosity and help…
So caring and supportive
To leave behind traditions, ceremonies…
Which I can hardly take ahead
The mental connect with you seems to have flown away with the wind
Like the flash of lightning
In the void of a black hole
The father of my children
Leaving me alone
You were like my guardian;
More than a lover, a partner in quest…
When you left my side:
Bereft of your physical self
The road ahead seems so long, with no desires left…
The trees and plants carry your smell,
The flowers, fruits, pond, fishes, birds and bees remind me of our common interests
And carry me ahead
Working with simple people around, leaving the elite
The last birthday celebrations' memories kept popping…
Instead of tears, they gave me courage
Instead of regret, they gave me gratitude
Vacuum can never be filled…
Carrying his love gave me three wonderful children
A lifelong companion
Now guides and perpetuates my thoughts…
He is physically absent
His spirit lives on… Jai Ho Umapati![1]

---

[1] Dr Rai Umapati Ray Father of Dr ,Mahoua Ray, Advocate Dr Talish Ray Bureaucrats Rai Mahimapati Ray & Husband of Prof (Dr) Kum Kum Ray

Art of Living

30th Aug 2024
Born in a family of bureaucracy,
Daughter of a Customs & Central Excise Officer (I.R.S.),
Wife of an Indian Police Officer (I.P.S.),
Mother of an Indian Administrative Officer (I.A.S.).
My maternal grandpa, a Tehsildar and City Magistrate,
From the British Raj to the freedom of our nation.
I learnt a lot of things...
Impressing is not inspiring,
Humility is inspiring,
Show-off is dilapidating,
Being a part of humankind is what is divine.
Now, after seven decades, I am often asked,
How do I live a happy, fulfilling life?
By being a good person!
Observation of others surprises me...
Am I an artist of life?
The realisation dawns...
My endeavours are to help ordinary people
Effectively meet their everyday challenges of life,
Deal with inevitable losses, disappointments, and griefs...
Bringing me a tranquillity of happiness and personal fulfilment.
Trying only to do what is right
Makes me feel synonymous with cherished personal ideals.
Goodness is available to anyone—
Rich or poor,
Educated or simple,
Monk, saint, or an ordinary family person.
Bringing action and desire in harmony with nature,
Mastering one's desires,
Performing one's duties,
Thinking clearly about oneself,
And one's relationships within the larger community of humanity,
Makes life move on...
Even with the vacuum of the loss of a life partner.
In gratitude,

Praying for serenity to accept what one cannot change,
Courage to change the things one can...
May be the taproot of self-management and modern psychology,
Leading to the art of living.

End of 2024

Whenever I go,
Conversations are only on A.I.
The one word keeping in every dialogue,
Whether get-together, discussion, or headline,
Putting fear in job seekers of losing employment.
Where machines will perform all cognitive functions
That are associated with our human brains,
May even exercise,
Girdling A.I. into reality.
Process of machine leading to A.I.,
So human capitalism.
The completism confounds us with misinformation,
To replace me with machine.
Concluding for,
With serious misuse or social blunders,
Until and unless there is gradual transition,
With A.I. labs, human experts, and government steps in,
Instituting a moratorium.
The imperfect has its own beauty,
While the perfect its flaws.
Great expectations may not always be met,
Magnificent obsessions may soon or slowly fade,
But hard times don't last forever.
All ends are eves of a new beginning.
So here's closing another chapter in our lives,
And opening a new one,
While we look before and after,
And rest content with what is.

In the Year 1995

Moving down from Nainital,
To the Naukuchiya,
My flesh is soaked in the mountain air.
Eyes linger on the hills around,
And my soul grows restless
With the desperation—
Why had I left it all and come down?
The eternal dilemma
Bids me calling.
Got sucked into the trodden path,
Forty minutes on the winding roads,
As the car slowed down
To yet another lake (*tal*) dangling.
These lakes had witnessed ages,
Had been part of glacial movements,
Left behind in the terminal mountains—
Corrie lakes,
Vandalised on the sides by malls
To draw nature,
Or tourists et al.
The crowd halts the car,
Steep upward drive
To yet another hill
In the vicinity of Nainital.
The drizzle tickles the skin,
The pink flowers and the green,
The blooms picture-perfect,
Get imprinted like pressed flowers
In my mental cards.
The descent makes it dizzy,
And my eyelids droop to overcome
The discomfort of it all.
The car slows down into
The valley beds,
And my eyes open to
A thousand pink lotuses

Floating over a lake,
Receiving raindrops in its bosom.
The round, big queen lotus
And the shaded pink lotuses
Stand tall above the waters amidst
The leaves, boastfully
Proclaiming—O ye who come thither,
I have impacted on you all.
Standing still, aloof with conceit,
Benign arrogance,
Royally above the leaves,
Proclaiming as it were,
O ye who connect hither—
Try and escape my charm.
But I was left dumbfounded.

Guru Shishya Parampara at Amity

Dedicated to my dear "Shishya" from Amity in the last two decades
In the classroom's vibrant lustre, my students stand to wish me their 'Acharya'—a seeker.
Listening to me, their mentor, with a steady hold,
Questioning, discussing stumbling blocks and barriers for new perspectives.
Still together, with our own hearts bound,
In their wisdom, they surely find
The light of knowledge in a race.
Each chapter a gift, a lifelong embrace.
With patience, I nurture each young mind with self-knowledge.
Becomes freedom—likes and dislikes—brook another's misery.
Gain acceptance and accessibility to the fold of good people.
A priceless treasure, one of its kind.
Every working day, I teach you
The wisdom that you imbue.
Make your teacher lifelong learners.
You too shape our futures, help us grow,
Keeping our hearts aglow.
Through trials and triumphs, I'll always be there,
Teaching you all with love and care.
For your dedication, we truly say,
God bless you, in every way.
So here's to the "Shishya", strong and true,
Who inspires in all we do.
With heartfelt gratitude, we humbly say,
You make my world fulfilling every day.

Indian Festivity with Colours

With a riot of colours spreading with the bloom of spring.
In the last phase of winter...
The mango trees loaded in gold.
The mulberry in green and purple.
Creeper and bougainvillea showing a myriad colourful spread from the ground to the head.
Holi arrives...
Giving statements of hugs, colours, and washing away differences from the canvas of everyone's life.
Vibrant hue of *gulal* denotes every blossom that enlightens our lives.
The *tamasha* on the crossroads with men soaked in alcoholic drinks, dancing and loafing without barriers or links.
As the day progresses...
Meeting and Holi Milans snatch time.
The distraction takes loners to another realm.
Yet life without a partner diminishes variance.
In the last decade of physical being,
Looking forward to the soul intertwining with the trees, breeze, flowers, a mosaic of hues from the theatre of living days (of hybrid colours).
Amrit...
Amidst the chaotic colours, the koel comes to sing, creating a symphony out of cacophony.
That sounds from engines and man-made machines.
The horn beeping on roads.
Motorcycles screeching...
From Holika Dahan (a day before Holi) night,
The traditional India honchoes free, the bank is loaded with cooking.
The letch times a factory 24x7 turning out handmade recipes traditionally handed down — *Dal Bhari, Puris, Kachories, Pua, Malpua,* along with fish fried and vegetables followed by mutton on a Holi brunch.
When the family, tribes, in-laws meet to drink *Thandai* and eat together.

The jest and togetherness from old to infants create an ambience unlike any other festival in *Hindu-istan.*
A time to connect to our grassroots connection of joint family days where the kitchen was one and every member shared the same.
Whether rich or poor, each in proportion contributed to the pot of healthy, freshly cooked food...
Flavours missing from market or restaurant-ordered food.
Soaked in water colours, dry *gulal* and *Tesu* flowers,
With the span of warm days flowing ahead.
The beginning of *Chait.*
The onset of summer.

Two Sides of the Same Coin

Love and hate are two sides of the same coin.
Hate comes when expectations are not met with whom one truly loves.
Love turns to hate, accepting impediments.
Little effort to resolve.
Love is not time-bound love when it differs from differences,
Or draws closer to negative thoughts.
Love is love when perceptions are optimistic,
Positive of a satisfied personality,
Yet deteriorates within an unsatisfied mind.
Blaming others rather than reflecting on the prime of self,
Without realising that blaming others disconnects relationships,
Leading to loneliness of the self.
Segregation is painful.
True love is a permanent mark that does not get disturbed,
As we accept that no human being is perfect and "Love alters not."
From the first breath to the last.
If this were contradicted,
Probably no one ever loved.
Love lost—can it ever be found?

Ganga Mai

An Ode to Celebrate 94 Years of Ginsberg and Kashi

In His "Promised Land"

Allen Ginsberg, disillusioned with America, brought himself and his partner, Peter Orlovsky, to Banaras—seeking an irrational approach to life.
An antidote to rationality.
To "make the refuse sanctified" (*Journal 8*).
The urge to sanctify and redeem what society has discarded as ugly, useless, or profane.
The world is holy;
The soul is holy;
The shit is holy;
The nose is holy;
The tongue and cock and heart and asshole holy!
He articulated his aesthetic and the ethnic artistic values.
From Judaism to Buddhism—there was a gradual change through experience.
He arrived in his "Promised Land": India—far from modern-day Israel, the historically acclaimed Promised Land.
"I am deliriously happy," he wrote. "It's my Promised Land."
Kashi: The Spiritual Land
In Varanasi, there evolved a shift in his attitude towards death.
Sitting for hours observing cremation at the Kanika Ghat in Varanasi, he witnessed and smelled the mortal flesh, seeing "the inside of the human body... the face cracked and torn, fallen off, the brains bubbling and burning."
Ginsberg admitted he was "amazed by the openness" and the visibility of death, "which is hidden and pondered and roughed and buried in a coffin in the West."
In Kashi—the Hindu holy city of the dead—the ghats lost their horror.
Living in a rented apartment on Dashashwamedh Street,
Ginsberg and his partner recorded the complex drama that played out before their eyes:
the dignity and deeply felt emotion with which a son lights his mother's pyre;

"the beauty of crowding, bathing nakedness" (*Journal 154*) of the devout Hindus;

the sheer energy of life in the midst of death—"was like burning away fear. I thought [it was] burning the dross inside me" (*Journal 125*), concluded Ginsberg.

I

The hills and forests around with Ganga gurgling,
Down in its youth, with gaiety.
The lone Sute surrounded by a cacophony of raindrops,
With solitary bird-chirps in broken rhythms.
A comfortable, luxurious bed at Roseate,
Nestled above Shivpuri in the lap of the Himalayas.
The divine gratitude envelopes,
Envelopes,
For bestowing a daughter,
A grandson,
Who spend their time and make my breath,
Every breath meaningful.
The gurgling, hyper, giddy-headed Ganga,
So much in love with the Lord of the Universe,
Shiv, all over the Himalayas,
Infuses the mute, spellbound believer
With abundance of satisfaction, gratification.
Ganga, you lure me
With your youthfulness,
Agility.
The green forested hills hold your hand,
Rising to be mountains
At the break of the day on every dawn.
From Gangotri to Devprayag, people
Eagerly line up on the ghats wherever they can for a dip.
At the dusk of every day,
When the sun sinks down,
Flames of Agni light up in diyas, lamps, eyes,
In thanksgiving, Ganga,
To your unending, ever-giving, generous charms.
Alaknanda and Bhagirathi wait to embrace you at Devprayag.
You choke them with your affectionate, magnetic charm,
And they mingle,
Submissively in joy,
Travelling with you.
I love to meet you at Ramjhula,

Take a dip in your embrace,
Then say goodbye till I meet you at
Varanasi—to me, Benares.
Expectant, you know my disposition,
And after my body leaves,
Will take my ashes to eternal rest.
At times,
You turn naughty and wild,
With flash floods,
Sweeping away whatever comes into your fold of mind.
A river dashing against its bank
In the August Indian monsoon in the Him-a-kayas,
Sullies its waters and fells the trees on the shore.

II

The Bhagirathi descends down serene
From Gomukh in Gangotri,
Receding
As the glacier retreats.
At Alaknanda she is so composed, with voluminous waves
Rolling playfully.
Brahmaputra—
The tumultuous, torrential, tearing in rage with passion—
Unites
His rage,
Her modesty.
Committed to each other,
They flow on as the revered Ganga,
Enfolding, assimilating,
Nurturing.
A young girl,
"Miss Please-All",
"Don't take my modesty as weakness," she warns.
As habitations
Touch her dignity,
She meanders, mesmerises,
Wreaks havoc to
Protect herself.
Indians place her on pedestals, worship her as a deity,
Yet fill her with
Sod and filth.
Hotel Raghunath,
Devprayag
Ramkund Resort,
Devprayag

III

Life and Death – Holding Hands by the Ever-Flowing Ghats of Ganga in Banaras (India)

We love the body, get attached to the soul; as the body fades, the attachment grows.
The years move on from childhood to youth, to adulthood, to old age…
Chances on Death
"Dirt thou art, to dirt returnest."
One's mind wanders through the lanes and by-lanes of Varanasi…
The dead mingle with the living…
One witnesses people carrying dead bodies to the ghats of the Ganges, to bathe them before placing them on their pyres to burn.
"Ganga Mai" cleanses them all—
both the living and the dead.
Swami Vivekananda's words resonate in my being:
"The day man will find that he never really dies; that his soul persists beyond death; he will have no fear of death."
Atma—the true self, the imperishable, the free, the eternal, unchangeable element,
subject neither to birth nor death, ever existing—
annihilates the fear of death,
pierces through layers of ignorance,
and lands us in the bliss and divinity of humanity.
At the ghats of the Ganges in Banaras,
the most ancient living city on the planet Earth…

In the light of the burning pyre
is the darkness of the night.
Creeping out are the Aghori sadhus,
clothed in ashes of the dead—
the cannibals of the holy ghats,
whom ordinary people fear and shun in disgust.
Manikarnika Ghat drives home so many schools of thought,
each leading me deeper into my quest.

The Aghoris are Shaivites, devoted to Shiva—
ascetics dwelling on and living off cremation grounds,
embracing death, devoting their lives,
using corpses as allies, transcending the duality of life and death.
They perform rituals involving sexual rites
and the consumption of substances
derived from death.
We see them through fantasy and exaggeration,
forgetting that their underlying principle
transcends the laws of purity
to realise ultimate non-duality.
A reality—
the ultimate, far from distinctions of "pure" or "impure"—
objects of fascination, both within and without.
John Lennon and Malcolm Foley, in their 1996 book,
referred to this as "death-related tourism"—
in simple terms, places associated with death.
But the question remains…
How can Varanasi, a place of veneration,
be a place of voyeurism?
Perhaps for some mindsets—
but not mine.
Varanasi
A holy city in India,
on the banks of the Ganga River,
known as
"Great Cremation Ground" (Eck, 1983: 30),
"Kashi, the Luminous",
"The Ancient Crossing",
"The Microcosm of the Universe" (Parry, 1994: 11)
A sacred landscape
where life and death coexist,
where multiple feelings intertwine
in timeless sanctity.

IV

Continuing .... Continuity...Of ancient civilization, along "Mai Ganga"

We love this body, and get attached to the soul,
As the body fades the attachment grows.
The years move on...
from childhood to youth to adulthood to old age .... Chances on Death:
'Dirt thou art to dirt returnest'
One's mind wanders through the lanes and bylanes of Kashi[2]....
The dead mingling happy with the alive.....
Witnessing people carry dead bodies to the ghats of the 'Ganga Mai' to bathe them before putting them on their pyre to burn.
'Ganga Mai' cleanses them all: both living and the dead.
Swami Vivekananda's words resonate in my being,
"The day, man will find that he never really dies; that his soul persists beyond death; he will have no fear of death."
'Atma': 'the true self' : the imperishable : the free : eternal unchangeable element : subject neither to birth nor death : ever existing ....
Annihilates the fear of death
pierces through layers of ignorance and lands us in bliss and divinity of humanity... At the ghats of 'Ganga Mai' in 'Kashi' ;
The most ancient living city on Planet Earth...........

In the light of the burning pyre;
In the darkness of the night

---

[2] Kashi – A holy city in India on the banks of the Ganga
"Great Cremation Ground" (Eck, 1983: 30)
"Kashi, the luminous",
The "Ancient Crossing",
The 'Microcosm of the Universe" (Parry, 1994: 11)
Religious sites where life and death co-exist and where multiple feelings are interspersed with a sacred landscape.

Creep out, the Aghori Sadhus clothed in smeared ashes; of the dead, the cannibals on the holy ghats: whom ordinary lot of people fear in disgust.

The Manikarnika ghat drives home so many school of thoughts that lead me to my quest. The 'Aghories' are Shaivites, devoted to Shiv;

Ascetics dwelling on and living off cremation ground;

Embracing death, devoting their life using corpse as allies transcending the duality of life and death.

To carry the rituals around sexual rites; Consumption of impure substance:

Derived from the death.

We see them in fantasy and exaggeration forgetting that their underlying principle, transcends laws of purity to realize ultimate non- duality.

A reality - the ultimate far from distinction as 'Pure" or 'Impure', Objects of fascination of both the Inside and Outside.

The Question lies …?

How can Kashi, a place of veneration, be a place of voyeurism? Maybe for a mindset…

Which isn't mine

V

The Glorious Month of August
With the glory of the Himalayas above Devbhumi,
Devprayag,
Rudra Prayag.
The clouds travel with me like companions, holding hands.
As the morn descends and the clouds ascend.
After a rainy night.
As one drives on the circumbulating road
With steep hills rising on one side
And the Ganga running thousands of feet below in its own carved valley.
The rush, the gush, the foliage, the boulders, brown and bleak,
The wild untended flowers, purple, white, grey.
The lantena thrives with yellow, red, pink, shaded, hanging from loose mud stones, pebbles, rocks embedded on the side.
Spurs.
The energy towards the divine
Longing to merge with the green, the brown, the dappled glory.
The Super Magnetic
Energy
That will assimilate mine,
Set me free.
Attain Moksh.

Nature

I

The Easterlis
The Westerlies
From East
From West
Bring…
One drying,
One saturating,
One takes away the moisture, creates wastelands,
One nourishes with rains, creates pastures, forest, and greens…
Like the Sun that rises in the East.
Bringing positive hopes
Sets in the West, spreading darkness…
The Cultures of the East
So contrary to the West.

II

At Netrahat Hill Station "Queen of Chhattis"

In the sal woods of Jharkhand
At Netrahat
Nature is bountiful.
Its inhabitants: survivors
Land covered Salwood forest.
Patched with pine.
This plateau indeed seems divine.
The red moraine
Those carpets
The terrace
Broken by boulders.
Raw stone in shades of brown refrain
Ore plateaus with bauxite jutting out in breaks.
As one winds
From lather
With armed guard in fright of what?
They say Naxalites fright
Infest
But to my naked
Eye
It seems to be an orderly "existence."
Without a single law imposing cop insight
People primitive
Plain, pensive, punny
Punky and pearly
Seen to move
About the parchment
With their pasturing pride.
Yet they say
Fear the Naxals'
Don't you see through the media
And news nerds
That paint them in colours not pleasing at all?
Naxals have
We made them

Deprive them of
Their lands.
Naxalites—people fighting for their habitants today
Freedom fighters of
Tomorrow.
We move on to Sunset Point through the bowl-shaped valleys.
Alive with virgin white
Pear blossoms
That takes our breath away.
Gone is the fear as the celebratory
Air smacks our face.
Native is so bountiful.
And that is
What is there?

III

At the Latehar,
Apprehensive as we arrive
We get closeted in our rooms
To the T.V. and the food, a part of hospitality boon.
We cab about the mosquitos
And all-pervading fear,
Armed Jawan spread
Here and there, everywhere—
As though a siege
We sleep fitfully,
In the terrorist area people called in Jharkhand
Praying to find our feet!
The Dawn breaks and the meaning is brought
It takes us out of bed for an early morning spirit's feel
Just as I look around I am beholden, beseeched
The gigantic 'Semal' (Cotton) trees
The big red flowers hoarded and amidst them
I see hundreds of bee hives in various sigen on it even spreading arms
Dripping with heavy
The colony of hives in such great multitype and size.
The fear vanishes.
I am free and enthralled, the gigantic cotton from tree
Red flowers, bee hives
All get painted on my canvas
In the album of my memories
When my son Rai Mahimapat Ray joined as DC Latehar

IV

An Ode to the Colors of Fall at Kansas, Missouri, USA (25th Oct 2019)

Leaves
Yellow, Green, Orange, Crimson, Red, Ochre, Pink, Brown, Olive,
Muddy, Purple, Gold
So many hues
Alive, vibrant,
Some lifeless, some dry.
To an Asian Indian eye (like mine)
As descend the Colors Fall in October, November.
I gasp, acclaim with open mouth and wider open eyes
What a feast to the senses.
Every time we drive by Lewinworth and Oakwood Drive,
I come back drunken,
Intoxicated in my soul.
When I call it a day,
Physically tired as I lie with my daughter and grandsons
On a high poster–king–sized bed, cushioned mattress, a foot-thick
Old
Body relaxing in comfort.
Something troubles my head.
What is nature trying to tell me?
Through a myriad of colours, spread out, many fold
The forest trees are a mosaic of colours scattered randomly.
And then I compare the colours of the forest to my own soul.
Some turn flaming with desire
Some turn green with envy
Some turn pale with fear
Some turn jaded and tired
Some turn muddy with confusion
Some turn brown with sweat and sunburnt
Some turn blue in desolation
Some turn purple and bruised
A mosaic of colour haphazardly, wildly spread
Through years of my life, fleetingly in my thoughts.
Then words burst out
On the paper in pen and ink, spread.

The colours of autumn
Fall
(Before snow descends and all lie underneath ashen snow
Tells me
Grieve not kummoo
If you have lived life, all colours
Before life ebbs out:
Like the leaves of fall
You will not lie unsung, forgotten by all.)

Philosophies

Wittgenstein

(26th April 1889 – 29th April 1951, Neuwaldegg, Vienna, Austria-Hungary)

Motto:

All that we learn that isn't just rustling and roaring can be said in three words:

What can be said can be said clearly. What cannot be said must be passed over.

Tractatus:

Tractatus addresses the relationship between thought, language, and the world.

Mind and World – Truth:

- **The correspondence theory of truth:** Thoughts and utterances are true when they correspond to the world.
- **Picture Theory:**
- We picture facts to ourselves; we picture a model of reality.
- A logical picture of facts is a thought.
- A thought is a proposition.
- **Language and Thought:**
- Language disguises thought.
- A proposition is a truth-functioning of elementary propositions.
- The limits of my language determine the limits of my thought.

Conclusion:

Tractatus is, in a sense, meaningless—it can show things that cannot be said.

Derrida

(Born: 15th July 1930 – 9th October 2004, El Biar, French Algeria)

Derrida: most controversial philosopher, protested, arrested. Born in 1930 – Algeria, sphenic Jew under French occupation.
Wrote over fifty books – often incomprehensible.
Critique of structuralism.
Kicks a subject & shows what is wrong with it.
What you have to do if you are a thinker is to take apart & reassemble it later.
Not to dismantle,
but to create it back together.
Construction & deconstruction.
Socrates' hemlock drunk:
Was it medicine or poison?
Yes, poison.
But for Socrates, it's a medicine for ending his life.
Fun to read – *The Postcard*: an ordinary person married for 30–40 years, successful in his own life.
He is happy to lie to you.
Why should he tell the truth?
Did translations of many Greek works.
What he does & writes is even known when he is wrong.
Better than most American thinkers.
Knowledge & logic.
New field: 'Critical Studies'.
Tormentor of other people.
Wrote in French: jokes & hilarious.
A genius when he says a spectrum of Marx – shady dog, starry – making fun of Marxism.
Museum for the Blind.
We want philosophers to be serious.
Was president at Cornell University.
Bridge in Cornell.
Subject: Why do you put up a net?
"University in the eyes of the people."

Wails Kinnar

I am alone.
I am a special creation of the divine.
I dance and sing.
I cry and cry.
I bless:
I am invited to bless;
Ceremonies remain incomplete if me and my tribe are not there to bless.
Am I heard?
Am I accepted?
Just because the male and the female have perspectives regarding my identity.
Who am I?
What do I have in mind?
What elements constitute the questions since the beginning of time?
Does anyone ever think
Of the responses I receive,
The environment I move in?
I look at the mirror; does it falsify truth?
I look again.
The mirror echoes back:
You are a distinctive being!
Why then is my image distorted and incomplete?
Identity begins with misconception.
How can I change that?
We keep pinning, looking at before and after.
That is our identity.
It is a distortion;
Understanding is misunderstanding.
An incomplete sentence.
I am a being, yet no one gives the colour of meaning.
Language abuses us,
Yet sex exploits.
I am a 'Kinnar'.
Can I be accepted?

Can my words speak?
A Kinnar wails to deaf ears?

The True Meaning of Equality

Prof. Laski – "Equality means, first of all, the absence of social privilege. In the second place, it means that adequate opportunities are laid open to all."
Absence of special privileges is a global phenomenon – because of a particular gender, female, biological.
On this basis, opportunities are not equally available, yet they are essential for sustainability.
Equality is the most valuable right of the people.
Since the French Revolution of 1789 – Liberty, Equality, Fraternity.
All men are born with equal rights.
The Declaration of the Rights of Man enshrined equality.
Egalitarians are believers in equality without gender differences.
Gender equality shapes how we live and allows anyone to cultivate all their talents.
For economic growth, we need human talent to foster creativity – and half of that talent is in women.
The gender gap is part of the challenge; it affects our planet, creativity, and the full potential of human talent.

I

'Culture' In Our Life Brings Joy In Various Contexts;
Complexities In Multiple Prospective
Training Our Minds In Mannerism And Texts.
Art The Intellectual Side Of Being Civilised.
Values, Norms, Symbols, Folklore, Idea And Religion.
In Its Three 'D Dimension'
Normative Makes Us Follow Ethical Norms;
Expressive, Expresses Music, Art, Normative
Making Our Lives Symbolic Of A 'Drama'
A 'Natak' Proposed By Destiny Or Divinity
Or On The Theory Of 'Karma' And 'Rebirth'.
Rangshalla Puts On Stage All The Above
Driving Messages Home Through 'Infotainment'
A Learning That Spreads The Enlightenment In Every Individual
The Publication Of Research Papers In This Volume May Bring
Forth The Areas Of 'Jeevan Shastra' Through Natya Shastra
Dramaturgy

A Tribute to F. Scott Fitzgerald

"Listen! The world only exists in your eyes."
"It was not an unhappy time," so you wrote.
Ye! Great Gatsby!
The protégée of 'Roaring Twenties'—crazy times,
Rock, Jazz, prosperity and penury,
Bootlegging and whoring,
Life was not at all boring.
Age of 'Excesses'—guilty of many things,
Pompous lifestyles, luxurious, kinks?
Wealth bred innovations.
By 1911, it issued its millionth patent.
Factory products flooded markets,
Obsessed with a new 'cult of celebrities,'
Unprepared to face the powerful backlash.
No 'Splendid Isolation,'
Chase your dream and display your wealth.
Ha? All was not right in 'This Side of Paradise.'
Buccaneers here, buccaneers there, buccaneers everywhere,
Mafia-raj, 'Art Deco,' bullets flying (fierce and fornicating), civil discord,
All hand in hand—'The Beautiful and the Damned.'
An age chronicled by Fitzgerald came cracking down.
Stock markets collapsed [1929], tumbled down.
It was the best of times that turned into the worst of times.
The chronicler became a victim of his time,
Bathtub gin and flaming youth,
Merry-go-round with ladies in gowns.
A penny saved was a penny wasted till 'The Camel's Back' was busted.
Came the hangover, dark and deep.
The War was a great relief.
It was a purge.
There was an urge
To save the world—what a surge!

Ye, Fitzgerald, you hardly lived long enough to paint it all.
For all the enchanted moments you saw,
You died an alcoholic at forty-four.